Contents

Oiilia

Bright Birds

Parrots are a family of brightly feathered birds. They are popular, or well liked, pets. In the wild, parrots are found in warm places all over the world, such as Australia, Central America, and South America. The parrot family is made up of around 300 different species, or kinds, of birds. The family includes parrots, macaws, parakeets, and cockatoos.

Parrots are not known only for their beauty. They are also known to be very smart. These bright birds are skilled at **mimicking** sounds, such as human speech. Some scientists even believe that parrots can learn the meaning behind the words they squawk.

These parrots are sun conures. Sun conures are about 12 inches (30 cm) long. These bright parrots come from South America.

Super Smart Animals

Parrots
Are Smart!

Leigh Rockwood

PowerKiDS
press™

New York

Published in 2010 by The Rosen Publishing Group, Inc.
29 East 21st Street, New York, NY 10010

First Edition

Editor: Amelie von Zumbusch
Book Design: Julio Gil
Layout Design: Ashley Burrell
Photo Researcher: Jessica Gerweck

Photo Credits: Cover, back cover (dolphin, horse, parrot, pig), pp. 5, 6, 9, 10, 14, 21 (main) Shutterstock.com; back cover (chimpanzee) Manoj Shah/Getty Images; back cover (dog) Courtesy of Lindsy Whitten; p. 13 Partridge Films LTD/Getty Images; p. 17 joSon/Getty Images; p. 18 Joseph Van Os/Getty Images; p. 21 (inset) Shutterstock.com; p. 21 Michael Goldman/Time & Life Pictures/Getty Images.

Library of Congress Cataloging-in-Publication Data

Rockwood, Leigh.
   Parrots are smart! / Leigh Rockwood. — 1st ed.
      p. cm. — (Super smart animals)
   Includes index.
   ISBN 978-1-4358-9376-4 (library binding) — ISBN 978-1-4358-9844-8 (pbk.) — ISBN 978-1-4358-9845-5 (6-pack)
   1. Parrots—Juvenile literature. 2. Parrots—Psychology—Juvenile literature. I. Title.
   QL696.P7R59 2010
   636.6'865—dc22
                                                2009036739

Manufactured in the United States of America

CPSIA Compliance Information: Batch #WW10PK: For Further Information contact Rosen Publishing, New York, New York at 1-800-237-9932

So Many Colors!

Parrots come in many sizes, from the 3-inch- (8 cm) tall buff-faced pygmy parrot to the 40-inch- (102 cm) tall hyacinth macaw. All parrots have strong, **curved** beaks. They have a pair of four-toed feet. Each foot has two toes that point forward and two toes that point backward.

Parrots can be many colors. For example, macaws' feathers can be blue, red, green, and yellow. You might think that this would make macaws stand out. However, a macaw's colorful feathers are hard to see against the colorful leaves, flowers, and fruits of the bird's **rain forest** home.

◄ There are several species of macaws. The parrot on the left is a hyacinth macaw, while the parrot on the right is a scarlet macaw.

Feet and Beaks

As other birds do, parrots get around by spreading their wings and flying. That is not the whole story, though. Parrots also depend on their feet. These birds use their feet for climbing around in trees. They pick up food with their feet, too. Parrots' feet are so strong the birds can even hold on to a branch while they hang upside down. This lets parrots reach hard-to-get fruits and nuts!

Parrots also use their strong beaks when they are climbing. They pull themselves up with their beaks. Though parrots do not fight often, they can use their sharp beaks to bite each other when they do.

A parrot's beak is very powerful. In fact, this bird's beak is so strong that it can break a person's finger!

▶

Flock Life

Parrots are social animals. This means that they enjoy living among other members of their species. Parrots live in groups called flocks. A flock can have from 10 to hundreds of members. Living in a group helps parrots watch out for **predators**.

Within their flock, parrots play and squawk at each other. They announce how they are feeling to the rest of the flock. Sometimes, they mimic each other. Flock members **groom** each other, too. This helps the members form close ties. Adult parrots generally form pair bonds. This means that they stay with the same **mate** for life and raise their young together.

◄ When they are forming a pair bond, parrots often groom each other. They most often groom each other's heads and necks.

A Parrot's Day

What is a wild parrot's day like? Around dawn, the flock wakes up and begins to squawk. These sounds tell where flock members are and how they are feeling. The sounds also let parrots know where their flock members are going for food. They even tell each other if there is danger nearby.

Parrots spend their day looking for food, feeding, grooming, and squawking. Parrots eat seeds, nuts, fruits, bugs, flowers, and tree bark. Some kinds of parrots use their strong beaks to break open hard nuts. At sunset, the flock meets again. The birds squawk about their return and then settle down for the night.

Different kinds of parrots like to eat different foods. White-fronted parrots, also known as spectacled Amazon parrots, eat mostly fruit.

▶

Baby Parrots

Parrots generally **breed** with the same mate throughout their lives. Female parrots lay between two and eight eggs. Baby parrots, or chicks, are nearly featherless for several weeks after they **hatch**. During this time, the father parrot brings food to the family while the mother looks after the chicks.

Both parents teach their chicks the flock's calls and how to stay away from predators. Parents also teach their chicks how to find food and water. Chicks move out of their parents' nest after they have grown and learned enough to live on their own. Depending on their species, parrots live between 10 and 60 years.

◄ Parrot chicks have soft feathers called down. These young African gray parrots have some white down, but you can also see their gray adult feathers growing in.

Parrots as Pets

People keep parrots as pets because these birds are social, smart, and beautiful to watch. Some can do tricks or mimic speech. African gray parrots are especially good at this. The most popular pet parrots are macaws, Amazon parrots, cockatiels, cockatoos, and parakeets.

Pet parrots can live for up to 60 years. They need lots of attention to stay clean, fed, and happy. Parrots that do not get enough exercise or become bored may pull out their feathers. They may even try to bite their owners. Parrots wake up early, so their owners should expect to be woken up by early-morning squawks.

Parrots require a lot of care. People must be sure that they can give a parrot the care it needs before buying one as a pet.

▶

Parrot Talk

The African gray parrot is one of the chattiest species of parrots. It can learn to mimic more than 700 words! Amazon parrots are also good mimics. This has made these birds popular pets.

Parrot owners and scientists have different ideas about why parrots mimic people. Some think that parrots turn to mimicry when they have no flock with which to **communicate.** People also disagree on how well parrots understand what they mimic. Sometimes a parrot seems to learn the connection between an object and its name. Other times, the parrot appears to like making sounds no matter what they mean!

◄ Some species of parrots are better mimics than others. Quaker parrots, like the ones shown here, are known for their talking skills.

Brainy Birds

Scientists have studied African gray parrots. They have found that these especially brainy birds do seem to understand some of the words they are taught.

Alex was an African gray parrot studied by a scientist named Irene Pepperberg. She found that Alex could do problem-solving tasks as well as dolphins and chimpanzees could. Alex could count to six. He could also **identify** and ask for 50 different objects. He could tell if an object was bigger, smaller, the same as, or different from another object. Pepperberg's work suggested that parrots really do know what they are talking about!

African gray parrots are among Earth's smartest birds. *Inset:* Pepperberg worked with Alex from 1977 until 2007.

▶

21

Parrots and People

Some parrot species are **endangered**, such as the night parrot and the Puerto Rican Amazon parrot. A few things can lead to a species becoming endangered. For example, people cut down forests and build houses where parrots live. This takes away the birds' **habitat**. People also take parrots from the wild and sell them as pets. If you are thinking of buying a pet parrot, make sure to get one that was born and raised in **captivity**.

Parrots are beautiful to watch. Now that you know more about these brainy birds, you will have something to squawk about the next time you see one!

Glossary

breed (BREED) To make babies.

captivity (kap-TIH-vih-tee) A place where animals live, such as in a home, a zoo, or an aquarium, instead of living in the wild.

communicate (kuh-MYOO-nih-kayt) To share facts or feelings.

curved (KURVD) Having a shape that bends or curls.

endangered (in-DAYN-jerd) In danger of no longer living.

groom (GROOM) To clean one's body and make it neat.

habitat (HA-beh-tat) The kind of land where an animal or a plant naturally lives.

hatch (HACH) To come out of an egg.

identify (eye-DEN-tuh-fy) To tell what something is.

mate (MAYT) A partner for making babies.

mimicking (MIH-mik-ing) Copying something else closely.

predators (PREH-duh-terz) Animals that kill other animals for food.

rain forest (RAYN FOR-est) A thick forest that receives a large amount of rain during the year.

Index

Web Sites

Due to the changing nature of Internet links, PowerKids Press has developed an online list of Web sites related to the subject of this book. This site is updated regularly. Please use this link to access the list: www.powerkidslinks.com/ssan/parrot/